THE

POTTER

Facts and trivia every fan should know

ELLIE DOWN

summersdale

THE UNOFFICIAL GUIDE TO HARRY POTTER

Copyright © Summersdale Publishers Ltd, 2005
Text by Ellie Down
Illustrated by Rob Smith

Reprinted 2005

Summersdale Publishers Ltd
46 West Street
Chichester
West Sussex
PO19 1RP
UK

www.summersdale.com

Printed and bound in Great Britain

ISBN 1 84024 476 3

Disclaimer: This book has not been approved or endorsed by J. K. Rowling, Bloomsbury or Warner Bros.

Contents

Warning:
This book contains spoilers!

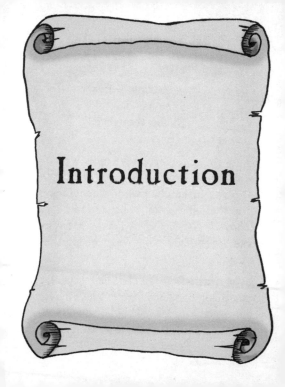

Introduction

Set against a captivating backdrop of magic and adventure, the characters created by J. K. Rowling are dynamic and real. They struggle with homework, friends, school bullies and relationships, all while fighting the ultimate battle between good and evil.

Harry Potter is everybody's hero. We wait with bated breath for each new story about his fascinating world, encouraging him to battle with Voldemort and his followers, rejoicing when he's happy and feeling his pain when he and his friends suffer.

Every Harry Potter fan has their favourite character and they know which house they themselves would belong to. Moreover we all share that secret wish that *that* letter arrived at our houses on our eleventh birthdays, heralding a flight into fantasy and friendship, Hogwarts and heroism, and whisking us away from our Muggle lives.

The phenomenally successful tales are packed with layers of detail and this handy guide will reveal everything you need to know, from plot summaries to character biographies, the lowdown on magical creatures and spells, to trivia from the books and the films. Also, don't miss our Hy-Potter-sis sections, outlining compelling ideas as to how the series will end.

Read on to learn the stories behind the stories and become an expert on the boy wizard everybody loves.

Harry Potter and the Philosopher's Stone

The Book

Harry Potter discovers that he is a wizard, famous in a world he never knew he was part of for defeating the powerful Dark wizard Lord Voldemort. He starts his first year at Hogwarts School of Witchcraft and Wizardry and makes friends (most notably Ron Weasley and Hermione Granger) and an enemy (Draco Malfoy). Together Harry, Ron and Hermione solve the mystery of the third-floor corridor and, after they complete a number of difficult tasks, Harry comes face to face with his parents' murderer, Lord Voldemort, who has spent the last ten years struggling to regain his powers. But Harry saves the Philosopher's Stone from Voldemort and becomes a hero all over again.

The idea for Harry Potter came to J. K. Rowling while she was travelling from Manchester to London. Being without pen or pencil meant that she couldn't write down any of her ideas and instead spent the four-hour train journey thinking intently about Harry and his world. More than 250 million copies of her books have been sold, and they have been translated into 62 languages, including Latin and Ancient Greek.

Harry James Potter

His birthday is 31 July and he has a lightning-shaped scar on his forehead, the only visible sign of the curse that should have killed him. He also has messy, jet-black hair like his father and vivid green eyes like his mother.

After his parents are murdered, one-year-old Harry is sent to live with his Muggle relatives, but it isn't until his eleventh birthday that Harry finds out why they've always treated him so badly: they fear and despise his magical heritage. He now lives between number four Privet Drive and Hogwarts.

Despite being a Gryffindor and not a Slytherin, Harry can speak Parseltongue (the language of snakes), a talent that he inadvertently picked up when Voldemort tried to kill him. He is the youngest Hogwart's student to play in the position of Quidditch Seeker in over one hundred years and, while he's not the smartest student in the school, he's brave, inventive and determined.

Friendship holds great value for him and he misses his classmates terribly during the holidays. Mrs Weasley is the only person to have hugged him like a mother, which makes him feel like part of her big, warm family.

Number Four Privet Drive

This is the very normal house in Little Whinging, Surrey, where Harry Potter grew up. Although Harry hates living with Aunt Petunia, Uncle Vernon and his cousin Dudley, his protection from Voldemort depends upon his spending at least part of his summers there – this protection was won by his mother Lily when she died to save him. He now has a bedroom upstairs, but for much of his life Harry slept under the stairs in a little cupboard.

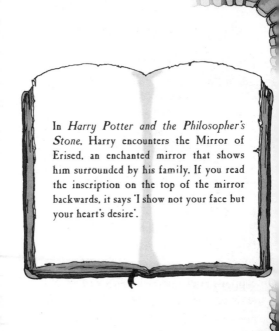

In *Harry Potter and the Philosopher's Stone*, Harry encounters the Mirror of Erised, an enchanted mirror that shows him surrounded by his family. If you read the inscription on the top of the mirror backwards, it says 'I show not your face but your heart's desire'.

Ronald Bilius Weasley

A very tall boy with ginger hair and lots of freckles, Ron is one of Harry's best friends and was also sorted into Gryffindor. His birthday is 1 March and he lives with his parents, Molly and Arthur, his twin brothers, Fred and George, and his little sister, Ginny, in The Burrow – a very scruffy house just outside the village of Ottery St Catchpole. His three older brothers, Bill, Charlie and Percy, have now all left home.

He is an expert at wizard chess, avidly supports the Chudley Cannons Quidditch team and has a terrible fear of spiders. As the youngest boy in a family of talented wizards, Ron has always struggled to gain recognition for his own talents and is thrilled but almost hysterically nervous by his appointment as Keeper of the Gryffindor Quidditch team. He proves his worth when he helps to win the cup in their fifth and sixth years. He's loyal and steadfast and never shies away from defending Harry or helping him fight Voldemort.

Wands

Wands – the instruments used to cast spells and charms – are made of wood with a special core, so that every one is unique and attuned to a particular wizard or witch.

Ollivanders' wands are all made with one of three powerful magical cores, and all three are represented in the wands of Harry, Ron and Hermione. Both of Ron's wands have a core of unicorn tail-hair, Hermione's has a dragon heartstring and Harry's has a phoenix tail feather.

The wood for each of their wands corresponds to the wood of their birth months, chosen by J. K. Rowling from a Celtic tree chart (Harry's is holly,

Hermione's is vine wood and Ron's second wand is willow).

Harry's wand is the brother wand to Voldemort's, which also has a feather from Fawkes the phoenix at its core. On the rare occasions when brother wands are forced to duel, an unusual reaction takes place, as seen in the altercation between Harry and Voldemort in *Harry Potter and the Goblet of Fire*.

The Film

Daniel Radcliffe, Rupert Grint and Emma Watson make their first appearances as Harry, Ron and Hermione. As J. K. Rowling worked very closely with the director, the changes in the film do not alter the plot of the book, nor do they disclose any information given in later books. However, some scenes had to be rewritten because of the time limit set on the length of the film – in fact, even though Rik Mayall had already filmed his scenes as Peeves the poltergeist, his part had to be cut completely.

J.K. Rowling insisted on an all-British cast for the Harry Potter films, although exceptions were made for Irish-born Richard Harris and Brendan Gleeson who played Dumbledore and Mad-Eye Moody respectively. American actors Rosie O'Donnell and Robin Williams were so eager to play parts that they offered to work for free, but so far they haven't been cast in any role. While Steven Spielberg was the first choice for director, he wanted Haley Joel Osment to play Harry and in the end Warner Brothers decided to offer the job to Chris Columbus of *Home Alone* fame.

Who will live happily ever after?

The friendship of the three main characters was sealed when Harry and Ron saved Hermione from the troll and she took the blame for their rule-breaking behaviour. However, will the bond be ripped apart as puberty and hormones set in?

The three friends are growing up, becoming more aware of their emotions and beginning to form romantic attachments. Despite the wild rumours regarding Harry's and Hermione's blossoming relationship, it's clear that, although they care for each other, their hearts are taking them in other directions.

Harry struggles with his feelings for Ginny, knowing that their relationship could damage his friendship with her brother Ron. But even after Ron accepts this romantic pairing, Harry has misgivings. As the only person to be possessed by Voldemort, Ginny can understand Harry's fears and is willing to fight alongside him as a member of Dumbledore's Army, but the more time they spend together, the more dangerous it will be for her.

Ron and Hermione won't admit their feelings for each other, though these feelings have been building for some time. Ron is wildly jealous of how close Hermione gets to Viktor Krum in their fourth year while Hermione is upset over Ron's relationship with Lavender in their sixth year.

In whatever direction their emotions take them, the three friends must also consider that they have committed themselves to fighting Voldemort and that there is the possibility that one or all of them might not live to see the last day of school.

Harry Potter and the Chamber of Secrets

The Book

After a strange meeting with Dobby the house-elf and a flying rescue by Ron and his twin brothers, Harry heads back to Hogwarts for his second year. At Hallowe'en they discover that the Chamber of Secrets has been opened and that enemies of Slytherin's heir should be on their guard. Everyone suspects Harry is the heir and the perpetrator of the mysterious attacks, but with Ron's help Harry finds the entrance to the Chamber, rescues Ginny, kills the Basilisk and destroys the diary left behind by the adolescent Lord Voldemort. Out of gratitude for Dobby's warning, he sets the house-elf free.

The name 'Voldemort' (with a silent 't') is taken directly from the French phrase '*vol de mort*', meaning 'flight of death'.

Lord Voldemort

Tom Marvolo Riddle changed his name to Lord Voldemort during his school years in rejection of his Muggle father and because the name wasn't sufficiently grandiose to suit his heinous ambitions. A direct descendant of Salazar Slytherin, Riddle opened the Chamber of Secrets while still at school, in the hope of completing Slytherin's work. Riddle/Voldemort, like Slytherin before him, believes in the supremacy of pure-bloods although part of his hatred of Muggles stems from his father's abandonment.

His campaign of terror appeared to end after his failed attempt to kill the infant Harry, whom he believed to have the power to destroy him following a prophecy by Professor Trelawney. He managed to avoid being completely destroyed when the killing curse rebounded but it is only years later, with the helping hand (literally!) of loyal servant Peter Pettigrew, that he regains physical form; one more snakelike and grotesque than before.

Referred to as You-Know-Who or He Who Must Not Be Named by all wizards except Harry and Dumbledore, Voldemort delights in the fear he instils and is willing to destroy whoever gets in his way in order to survive.

Hogwarts School of Witchcraft and Wizardry

Founded over a thousand years ago by the four cornerstones of the magic world, Hogwarts is where British and Irish witches and wizards learn the art of magic. It is a complex and mysterious place where ghosts glide along the corridors, doors and stairs change place without warning and the ceiling of the Great Hall is enchanted to look like the sky outside.

The school is bewitched to give it the appearance of a dangerous old ruin, thus ensuring its protection from Muggles, and it is surrounded by other spells that guard against encroachment by magical means. Ordinary electronic equipment such as bugs can't be used on the grounds because of these spells and only magical cameras will function.

Hogwarts is full of hidden passageways, such as the one that leads from the statue of the one-eyed witch on the third floor to Honeydukes in Hogsmeade. The school also has secret rooms, like the Room of Requirement where the students hold their defence association meetings and find it equipped with every book and device they need, and where Dobby finds a house-elf-sized bed and Butterbeer antidotes when he takes fellow house-elf Winky there to sleep off her hangovers.

Students gather in the Great Hall for the beginning and end of each school year, and for all their meals during the year. They eat at separate house tables, each of which has an equivalent on the ground below where the house-elves place the food for each meal and then magically transport it to the floor above. The Hall is always decorated beautifully for each special occasion, such as Hallowe'en, when bats fly around and pumpkins are used as candleholders.

The word 'Muggle' was included in the *Oxford English Dictionary Online* on 13 March 2003 and can now also be found in the latest edition of the *Oxford Dictionary of English*.

Aunt Petunia

Aunt Petunia is blonde and skinny with an abnormally long neck, which makes it easier for her to poke her nose into other people's business.

She hated her sister because their parents gave Lily more attention and especially because they were proud of Lily being a witch. When she found Harry on her doorstep she reluctantly agreed to give him a home, although she was never happy living with a wizard. She and her husband Vernon believed that if they ignored Harry's magical side, it would simply fade away. They are horrified when Harry discovers the truth and each summer when he returns home, they are tormented by their fear that the neighbours will see Harry perform magic. Their son Dudley is a spoiled bully who is nervous of Harry's abilities after a number of unfortunate encounters with magic.

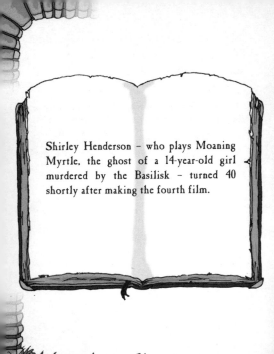

Shirley Henderson – who plays Moaning Myrtle, the ghost of a 14-year-old girl murdered by the Basilisk – turned 40 shortly after making the fourth film.

The Film

Chris Columbus was the director for this film as well as the first and again remained faithful to the plot of the book. He did, however, add an extra scene during the closing credits that shows Professor Lockhart, played by Kenneth Branagh, suffering the results of the backfiring memory charm.

All of the scenes that included Professor Dumbledore were filmed first to take Richard Harris's deteriorating health into account. Richard died on 25 October 2002 from Hodgkin's disease, shortly before *Harry Potter and the Chamber of Secrets* was released.

Houses

Helga Hufflepuff, Rowena Ravenclaw, Godric Gryffindor and Salazar Slytherin named the four houses of Hogwarts after themselves and entrusted the Sorting Hat with the task of dividing the students into the house that best suits their abilities. Gryffindors are known for their bravery and courage, while Hufflepuffs are loyal and hard-working. Ravenclaws are often the most intelligent of students and although Slytherin house usually takes only pure-blood wizards and witches, those with sly, manipulative and cruel tendencies are also accepted.

Each house has its own tower, with a common room and bedrooms for its students. The warm and cosy common room overlooking the Forbidden Forest is where Gryffindor students spend most of their free time, doing homework or playing games such as wizard chess and gobstones. The Slytherins' common room is a dark, green-lit underground room with elaborately carved furniture that reflects the Slytherins' showy arrogance.

What does Aunt Petunia know?

Despite not wanting to have anything to do with the wizarding world, Petunia is tied to Harry as a result of her sister's sacrifice for her son. The manner of Lily's death invoked ancient magic that gives Harry protection from Lord Voldemort, as long as he returns regularly to live with his aunt, no matter how short a time he spends in her home. By agreeing to give Harry a home, Petunia sealed a pact with Dumbledore and even though she wants to throw Harry out after the Dementor attack in *Harry Potter and the Order of the Phoenix*, she backs down when she receives Dumbledore's Howler. She knows about Dementors and Azkaban, and she is aware – not to mention afraid – of the implications of Lord Voldemort's return, indicating that she is not completely ignorant of her nephew's world. But exactly how familiar is she with the wizarding community? Her genuine terror seems to run deeper than would be expected of a Muggle overhearing a conversation about Dementors (she claims to know about them only after eavesdropping on Lily and James). Could it be that she herself is a witch?

In September 2002 a school for witchcraft and wizardry opened in southern Austria. During the six-term course, students can take classes in potions, history of magic and meditation as well as astrology and divination, working towards a Sorceror's Diploma.

Harry Potter and the Prisoner of Azkaban

The Book

Harry begins his third year with the knowledge that Sirius Black, a convict from Azkaban, has escaped. He later overhears that Black is his godfather and the one who betrayed his parents to Voldemort. After several disturbing encounters with Dementors Harry convinces Professor Lupin to teach him the Patronus Charm. Harry, Ron and Hermione meet Black, but find out that he was framed by another friend, Peter Pettigrew, who has been hiding as Scabbers the rat and is Voldemort's servant. Hermione and Harry travel back in time, save themselves from the Dementors, rescue Black and set him free on Buckbeak the Hippogriff.

Alfonso Cuaron, the director of *Harry Potter and the Prisoner of Azkaban*, makes a number of appearances in the film; as a wizard in the Leaky Cauldron and in a portrait on Hogwarts' walls. His daughter, Tess Bu Cuaron, is the baby in the portrait next to the Fat Lady's at the entrance to the Gryffindor common room. Chris Columbus also cast his daughter in the films he directed: Eleanor Columbus plays Susan Bones, and his other children have background parts.

Remus Lupin

One of James Potter's best friends, Lupin has a youthful appearance but is visibly fatigued by the burden of being a werewolf. Aware of Lupin's situation, Dumbledore allowed him to attend school as a teenager and even arranged to have the Whomping Willow planted to hide the secret passage to the Shrieking Shack, Lupin's refuge during his monthly transformations. The Shrieking Shack was rumoured to be the most haunted house in Britain because of the howls and screeches heard by the terrified inhabitants of Hogsmeade every month when Lupin needed to go into isolation.

When James Potter and Sirius Black, together with Peter Pettigrew, found out

Lupin's secret, they became Animagi to keep him company. The Ministry of Magic insists that all Animagi be registered with them as the magic involved in the process is very complicated and needs to be monitored. The close-knit group, however, kept their activities hidden, making a pact which cemented their friendship and made Sirius's apparent betrayal all the more hurtful.

Dumbledore later appointed Lupin teacher of Defence Against the Dark Arts during Harry's third year, a position which Lupin filled very well until his secret became known. During that year, Lupin's transformations were prevented by a special potion brewed by Snape.

Hogsmeade

Hogsmeade is the only completely magical community in Britain. This quaint village, with its thatched cottages and unusual shops, is very popular with teachers and students at Hogwarts, although only those students in the third year or above and with permission from a guardian may visit. Children love Zonko's Joke Shop and Honeydukes sweetshop, while anybody who needs any wizarding equipment can go to Dervish and Banges.

After a hard day shopping for Dungbombs and Sneakoscopes, everybody drops in at the Three Broomsticks pub for a big mug of warm Butterbeer, a favourite tipple amongst wizards. It tastes rather like butterscotch and isn't strong enough to have an effect even on thirteen-year-old students. The rather curvy landlady Madam Rosmerta, on the other hand, certainly does have an intoxicating influence on the young wizards.

Hermione Jane Granger

Sorted into Gryffindor, she has big, bushy brown hair, large front teeth and is an extremely talented and intelligent witch who has yet to find a spell that can defeat her. Before coming to Hogwarts she had read every book on the syllabus and several more besides, which means that she knows more about the school than even the teachers. Born of Muggle parents, her birthday is 19 September and she's always on hand to solve any mysteries and regularly (though not always willingly) helps Harry and Ron with their homework.

She's obsessed with studying and getting good marks, and even travels through time to take on extra classes in her third year. She is particularly annoyed at Harry's new-found skills in Potions in their sixth year because it's the first time someone has beaten her to the top of the class. Kind-hearted and with a keen social conscience, one of her recent hobbies is SPEW (Society for the Promotion of Elfish Welfare), which she herself set up in her fourth year after learning of the working conditions for house-elves.

Dementors

Dementors have one purpose: to drain all the happiness and hope out of their victims. Their *coup de main* is the Dementor's Kiss, which they perform to suck the soul from the person they want to completely destroy. They hide their bony hands and their blank faces underneath flowing black cloaks and can fly through the air, making escape from them extremely difficult.

As the guards at Azkaban, the Dementors were under the control of the Ministry of Magic, but they changed their allegiance to Voldemort after his return as he could offer them more victims and fewer restrictions.

Eating chocolate helps to get rid of the feelings of hopelessness induced while the Patronus Charm, an advanced form of magic, can be used to fight off a Dementor. Together with the incantation *Expecto Patronum*, the caster must concentrate on their happiest memories, thereby creating a projection of hope and the desire to survive, which in turn produces the Patronus or guardian.

Harry's Patronus takes the form of a stag, which is also the shape his father took as an Animagus.

Alfonso Cuaron spent six months trying to create the Dementors for the film because he wanted puppets which could be filmed underwater. However, this idea was too difficult to realise and had to be abandoned. The Dementors were instead created using computer generated technology – although, as a tribute to his original idea, there is ethereal, underwater-style music playing in the scene with the Dementor on the train.

Boggarts

In their first Defence Against the Dark Arts lesson with Professor Lupin, Harry and his classmates came across one of these shape-shifting creatures, hiding in a wardrobe in the staff room. Boggarts can also be found under beds or in small cupboards, and they attack by taking on the form of the victim's worst fear. In order to get rid of a Boggart, you must use the incantation *Riddikulus* while thinking of a way to turn your greatest fear into an object of ridicule. Laughter is the best way to make a Boggart vanish. It's advisable to fight one of these creatures with several other people so that the Boggart will be confused as to what shape it should take.

Pets

Hogwarts students are allowed to bring a cat, an owl or a toad to school with them. Owls are considered the most useful pets as they carry post and messages, and Harry has a beautiful snowy owl named Hedwig, a birthday gift from Hagrid. Hermione has a huge, ginger half-cat, half-kneazle called Crookshanks, whom she purchased before their third year, and who took a distinct dislike to Scabbers the rat.

Ron brought Scabbers to school as his pet even though, strictly speaking, rats are not on the list of acceptable animals to bring to Hogwarts. After Scabbers's return to Voldemort, Sirius gives Ron a tiny (and very enthusiastic) owl called Pigwidgeon, or Pig for short.

Neville's great-uncle Algie gave him his toad Trevor as a 'reward' for having magical ability – Neville had bounced down the garden after his great-uncle was distracted by meringues and dropped him out of an upstairs window. The ever-forgetful Neville keeps losing Trevor but is reunited with him each time.

Honeydukes

Honeydukes, the wizarding sweetshop with branches in both Diagon Alley and Hogsmeade, supplies every wizardly sweet imaginable. They sell normal sweets such as chocolate and nougat, as well as more unusual ones like Bertie Bott's Every-Flavour Beans (jelly beans with flavours such as chocolate, rhubarb and vomit), Fizzing Whizzbees (sherbet balls that make you levitate) and Jelly Slugs. Cockroach Cluster and blood-flavoured lollipops are just some of the other sweet delicacies you can find.

A wizard favourite is Chocolate Frogs, which move like real frogs and come with collectible cards. Harry's first card is of Dumbledore and it was in the description on the reverse where Harry discovered a clue to the meaning of the Philosopher's Stone.

The Weasley twins invent sweets with even more special effects such as Fainting Fancies, Nosebleed Nougat and Canary Creams, although these are more of the practical joke variety (and also help you to get out of class and avoid exams).

The Film

A slightly darker film than the first two, *Harry Potter and the Prisoner of Azkaban* reflects the more sombre feel of the book. The only major change to the story is the portrayal of the Patronus Charm. In the book, a Patronus is shown as an animal that charges at the Dementors but in the film they are portrayed as shields of light that emanate from the caster's wands. There is also an extra scene where Harry and Professor Lupin discuss both his parents, whereas in the book they only talk about James Potter.

Who else is going to die?

All signs point to a member of the Weasley family. They're decent, honest and believe in doing the right thing. Mr Weasley has already been attacked while both Ron and Ginny have faced Voldemort at various times. It is possible that Ron will not live to the end of the seventh book, partly because, as Harry's best friend, he is often in the firing line. Also, at Christmas in their third year, Professor Trelawney claimed that the first to rise from a table of thirteen would be the first to die – Harry and Ron both rose at the same time. Although Professor

Trelawney's unfocused attempts to predict the future often fall flat, she has had two real prophecies, so there is a possibility that this 'prediction' may one day be realised.

Harry Potter and the Goblet of Fire

The Book

The friends attend the Quidditch World Cup during the holidays and Ron is jealous when Hermione goes to the Yule Ball with Viktor Krum. Harry is scandalously selected as the fourth contestant in the Triwizard Tournament and at the end of the third task is transported to a graveyard, when he and Cedric Diggory take hold of the cup together. Voldemort murders Cedric and uses Harry's blood in a ritual to regain a body. They duel but Harry manages to escape and get back to Hogwarts to raise the alarm. It is then that he discovers that the new Defence Against the Dark Arts teacher is an impostor and a Death Eater. Harry gives his winnings from the tournament to Fred and George to set up their joke shop.

Children have more power than they realise – several publishers, including Penguin and Harper Collins, had turned down the manuscript for *Harry Potter and the Philosopher's Stone* before 8-year-old Alice Newton convinced her father, Bloomsbury chairman Nigel Newton, to get her more chapters to read. And Richard Harris took the part of Dumbledore in the first two films after his 11-year-old granddaughter Ellie threatened to never speak to him again.

Severus Snape

Professor Snape has lank, greasy black hair, a hooked nose and cold black eyes, and demonstrates many of the typical Slytherin values. His relationship with Harry has been ambiguous to say the least, and this is reflected in the history he shares with Harry's parents: James Potter teased him mercilessly at school, then later saved his life; and some believe Snape was in love with Lily.

Fascinated with the Dark Arts from a young age, he became one of Voldemort's Death Eaters and has the Dark Mark on his left forearm. Before Voldemort's apparent defeat and disappearance, Snape left the Death Eaters and became a member of the Order of the Phoenix, dedicated to fighting the Dark Lord. He returned to Hogwarts, where Dumbledore trusted him with the job of Potions teacher. However, his real ambition is to be the Defence Against the Dark Arts teacher, despite the fact that the position seems to be cursed. Indeed, after killing Dumbledore he becomes the sixth DADA teacher in as many years whose position at Hogwarts comes to an abrupt end.

Paranormal Creatures

Hogwarts has several resident ghosts. These silvery-grey creatures float through the school, going about their daily 'deaths', communicating with the students in much the same way they did when they were alive.

Sir Nicholas de Mimsy-Porpington is Gryffindor's ghost and explains to Harry that he became a ghost because he feared death. Nearly Headless Nick has tried to join the Headless Hunt several times but because his head is still attached to his body, albeit by a small piece of skin, his application is always refused.

Hufflepuff's ghost is the Fat Friar and Slytherin's ghost, the Bloody Baron, is a haggered-faced horror covered in blood who scares even Peeves the poltergeist.

Peeves is a mischievous spook, and constantly plays pranks on the teachers and students. The first time Peeves ever obeyed a student was when he picked up the baton from Fred and George Weasley to make Professor Umbridge's life difficult after their departure.

Professor Binns teaches the History of Magic class and is just as boring in his ghost form as he was during his life, which he left without changing his routine or even noticing.

Hogwarts Express and Platform Nine and Three-Quarters

On 1 September each year the Hogwarts Express departs from platform nine and three-quarters full of witches and wizards eager to begin at or return to Hogwarts. The large red steam engine makes its way through the countryside and arrives at its one and only stop, the station in Hogsmeade.

Wizards have taken many precautions to ensure that no Muggle could accidentally find the platform in London's King's Cross station and the most notable of these is how to access it. Being careful to avoid Muggle attention, those wishing to find the platform must walk straight through the barrier between platforms nine and ten to find themselves on the other side, next to the departing train.

Once the students get to Hogsmeade, first-years take boats across the lake to the castle while all others are then transported to the school in Thestral-drawn carriages. Thestrals are winged, skeletal creatures with dragon-like heads that can only be seen by those with some experience of death.

Draco Malfoy

Draco is of pure-blood heritage, closely related to Sirius Black through his mother, Narcissa. He picked up his hatred of Muggles from his father, Lucius, a Death Eater. He has short white-blonde hair and blue eyes in a sharp, pointed face, and is never seen without his two 'bodyguards', Crabbe and Goyle.

Draco is proud of his Slytherin tendencies and willingly follows the Dark Arts and Voldemort, making him a natural enemy of Harry's. Draco was inadvertently responsible for Harry being made Seeker of the Gryffindor Quidditch team, while himself becoming the Slytherin Seeker only after his father bought expensive broomsticks for the whole team. Although he is a good flyer from years of practice at home, he does not have the same raw talent as Harry. A member of Umbridge's Inquisitorial Squad (set up by the professor as a means of spying on other students), he eagerly does whatever he can to undermine Harry and Dumbledore and regularly insults both Ron and Hermione.

After being given a special task by Voldemort in his sixth year, Draco finds a way to bring Death Eaters into Hogwarts, but he runs from the school after failing to kill Dumbledore.

Society

The people in Harry Potter's world are divided into those with magical abilities and those without. Those who can perform magic are called witches and wizards and can be of pure-blood or half-blood heritage.

Pure-bloods are proud of their ancestry and tend to look down on others. They are particularly scathing of 'half-bloods' – those with a non-magical person on their family tree – calling them 'Mudbloods'. Because pure-blooded wizards only marry and reproduce with other pure-bloods, their numbers are dwindling. Sirius was the last surviving member of his family, although he had been disowned when he ran away from home.

Death Eaters are usually from pure-blood families who share Voldemort's hatred of Muggles and love of cruelty and chaos. They consider themselves to be superior to all others; even other pure-blooded families who don't follow Voldemort, such as the Weasleys and the Longbottoms.

Neither Squibs nor Muggles are able to perform magic at all, but Squibs do have magical parentage (whether half-blood or pure-blood) while Muggles go about their lives completely oblivious to magical occurrences in their country.

Quidditch

Quidditch is a very popular and fast sport with seven rules and more than seven hundred possible fouls. A team consists of seven players on broomsticks: three Chasers, who work together to get a football-sized red ball, the Quaffle, through one of the three hoops at one end of the oval pitch (scoring is worth ten points each time); a Keeper, to stop the other team's Quaffle from getting through; two Beaters to stop the two vicious balls called Bludgers from knocking their teammates off their broomsticks; and a Seeker, who must catch the tiny golden Snitch to score 150 points and end the game. Once the Snitch is caught, the team with the most points wins.

Held every four years since 1473, the most recent Quidditch World Cup took place in Britain, with the final match between Bulgaria and Ireland. Harry, Ron and Hermione watched from the top box as Ireland won, although Bulgaria's Viktor Krum caught the Snitch, which proves that catching the Snitch doesn't always guarantee a win, it simply signals the end of the match.

Harry Potter, Daniel Radcliffe and J. K. Rowling all have birthdays in July.

The Unforgivables

Punishable by imprisonment in Azkaban, the three Unforgivable Curses are regularly used by Voldemort and his Death Eaters.

Although he is supposed to teach only the counter-curses, Mad-Eye Moody teaches Harry and his friends these illegal curses in their fourth year.

The Cruciatus curse – the curse with the incantation *Crucio* is used to inflict extreme pain on its victim, as a form of punishment or to gain information.

The Imperius curse – the incantation *Imperio* is used to control the actions of the person it is set upon. Only very strong-willed wizards have the power to resist this curse.

The Killing curse – *Avada Kedavra* is considered the worst of the three curses, as it kills whomever the spell is cast upon and cannot be avoided or reversed (except in one very famous case).

Wanting to learn more about his leading actors, Alfonso Cuaron asked the three youngsters to write a short essay from the point of view of their characters. Daniel Radcliffe wrote a one-page essay, Emma Watson gave in an eleven-page piece and Rupert Grint didn't hand in anything at all, claiming that was exactly what Ron would have done.

Is Voldemort as powerful as everyone thinks he is?

Although it is widely believed that there is no escape from the Killing curse, Harry has survived it twice: the first time because of his mother's sacrifice and the second because of the unusual reaction brought about when two brother wands are forced to duel. Voldemort survived when the curse rebounded upon him because he had divided his soul and hidden the separate pieces to ensure that he would never suffer a mortal death. He had learned about this very Dark magic while still at school, proving that he sought power and feared death even then, yet at the height of his strength he overlooked a very important factor; the magic that Lily's sacrifice invokes protects Harry at the moment of the curse and also prevents him from even touching Harry's skin. Despite Voldemort's undeniable power, his actions prove that this power is flawed and show that he has weaknesses which could be used against him.

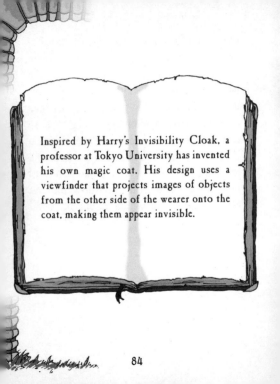

Inspired by Harry's Invisibility Cloak, a professor at Tokyo University has invented his own magic coat. His design uses a viewfinder that projects images of objects from the other side of the wearer onto the coat, making them appear invisible.

Harry Potter
and the
Order of the
Phoenix

The Book

Harry uses magic (illegally) against a Dementor but Dumbledore defends him at the disciplinary hearing and he is cleared of all charges. Professor Umbridge is the new Defence Against the Dark Arts teacher and Harry, Ron and Hermione set up 'Dumbledore's Army'. Harry and the Weasley twins are banned from playing Quidditch but Ron becomes the new Keeper and wins the cup for Gryffindor. Harry gets his first kiss from Cho Chang and is then lured to the Ministry of Magic by Voldemort. Sirius and the Order of the Phoenix come to rescue him, but Sirius dies in the Department of Mysteries. Dumbledore rescues Harry and tells him of the prophecy.

One of the most popular range of sweets in the wizarding world, Bertie Bott's Every-Flavour Beans are now available for Muggles to try. The Jelly Belly Candy Company, based in the US, sells boxes of the treats, which include flavours such as toasted marshmallow, spinach, dirt and 'booger'.

The Cursed Position

The position of Defence Against the Dark Arts teacher at Hogwarts has been cursed ever since Lord Voldemort was refused the appointment. While all the teachers have been very different in style and temperament, none have stayed longer than a year and some were in the service of Voldemort himself: Professor Quirrell was possessed; Mad-Eye Moody was actually Barty Crouch Junior in disguise; and Snape was the Dark Lord's spy. Professor Umbridge refused to teach the practicalities of defence and left after an encounter with a herd of centaurs while Professor Lockhart is in St Mungo's Hospital recovering from the effects of the memory charm (the only spell he knows). Professor Lupin was the only one to teach the students anything of value.

Dumbledore's Army

Harry and his friends set up Dumbledore's Army in reaction to Professor Umbridge's decision to teach only theory in her Defence Against the Dark Arts class. Meeting in secret, the group endeavours to learn the charms and spells that will help to protect them from Voldemort and his followers. Neville, in particular, is eager to learn and improves greatly under Harry's tutelage. The students are told of the time and date of each meeting by means of coins that look like ordinary Galleons but which have been enchanted by Hermione. When Umbridge catches the students, Dumbledore takes the blame for the illegal club, saving the students from punishment.

Sirius Black

Sirius has unruly dark brown hair and gaunt features, and as an Animagus he can transform into a large black dog. Of pure-blood heritage, Sirius was best friends with James Potter, and because he was James' and Lily's Secret-Keeper everyone believed he was responsible for their deaths. Despite proving his innocence to Harry, Sirius was still wanted by the Ministry of Magic for mass murder. He was a member of the Order of the Phoenix before his imprisonment, and after his escape he allows his family home at number twelve Grimmauld Place to be used as the Order's headquarters.

Haunted by his years in prison and his inability to move around the wizarding world freely, Sirius became bitter and angry but always loved his godson and tries to support him. It is he who gives Harry his much-envied Firebolt and the required permission slip so that he can visit Hogsmeade. He later dies protecting him from Voldemort.

Ministry of Magic

The Ministry of Magic is the wizarding body that is the equivalent of the Muggle government. The Minister for Magic is Cornelius Fudge, who is rarely seen without his lime green bowler hat and who consistently ignores Dumbledore's warnings that Voldemort has returned.

The entrance to the Ministry is an out-of-order telephone box in a quiet run-down street in London; you just need to dial 62442. The main hall is very long, with a dark floor and enchanted blue ceiling, and the Fountain of Magical Brethren is at the end. The Ministry has several departments such as the Department of Magical Transportation (which regulates the Floo Network), the Department of

Magical Games and Sports, and the secretive Department of Mysteries.

The Department of Magical Law Enforcement includes the Misuse of Muggle Artefacts, where Mr Weasley works. Fascinated by plugs and batteries, Mr Weasley is in his element sorting out regurgitating toilets and shrinking doorkeys.

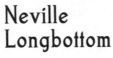

Neville Longbottom

Neville is from a pure-blood family and was sorted into Gryffindor in the same year as Harry. He has a small round face and a very nervous disposition but is very talented at Herbology, the study of plants. He is petrified of Professor Snape who dislikes him almost as much as he does Harry. Yet it was Neville's bravery that won the House Cup for Gryffindor in his first year and he defends Harry when others think the celebrated boy wizard is just looking for attention. Determined to improve his skills in Defence Against the Dark Arts, Neville joins Dumbledore's Army and takes part in the fight against Voldemort in the Ministry of Magic. He also answers the DA's call when the Death Eaters attack the school.

He lives with his grandmother but visits his parents in St Mungo's Hospital for Magical Maladies and Injuries. They were Aurors and members of the original Order of the Phoenix who were tortured to the point of insanity (with the Cruciatus curse) by Voldemort's followers.

Because Neville was born in July and his parents had also challenged Voldemort three times, he could have been the person referred to in Professor Trelawney's prophecy, but Voldemort saw the half-blood boy as more of a threat and chose to attack the Potters.

Photos and Portraits

Photos in the wizarding world are developed in a special potion, so that the images take on the mannerisms of the people in the picture. They cannot communicate with people outside of the photo, whereas portraits are created with special paint that allows the subjects to converse with others. Portraits guard the entrances to the four Hogwarts houses and don't allow access without the correct password. The walls of Dumbledore's office are covered with paintings of former Headmasters, who are duty-bound to serve the present Headmaster. Because the Headmasters are well known they have portraits in other establishments and can move freely between them.

In Germany, fans were so eager to read *Harry Potter and the Goblet of Fire* that they translated the book themselves. Over a thousand fans took a section each and posted the translations on a dedicated website, agreeing to read other pieces only after translating their own segment. Carlsen, the publisher responsible for the official German translation, insisted on the website being shut down. The fans didn't learn their lesson, however, and used the same technique to translate *Harry Potter and the Order of the Phoenix*.

Classes and Qualifications

Hogwarts students have to take exams every year, just as Muggle students do. At the end of their fifth year, all students have to take their first set of wizarding qualifications – OWLs. Ordinary Wizarding Levels are taken in every subject and often consist of a theory and a practical paper. The students then select the subjects they wish to study further and at the end of their seventh year, they sit their NEWTs (Nastily Exhausting Wizarding Tests). Divination and Transfiguration are just two subjects that may be taken to NEWT level: Divination is the art of seeing into the future using tea leaves, crystal balls and star charts and can be a rather vague subject, while Transfiguration requires absolute precision and skill.

The teachers of the two subjects couldn't be more different: Sybill Trelawney has taught at Hogwarts for more than sixteen years and has only had two real prophecies in that time, and Minerva McGonagall is an Animagus who can transform into a tabby cat and is one of the strictest teachers in the school. She is a close ally of Dumbledore's and, as head of Gryffindor house, keeps a close eye on Harry and his friends.

The Leaky Cauldron

The Leaky Cauldron, run by a toothless and extremely wrinkled old man named Tom, is a very famous inn - in the magic world. Muggles, if they see it at all, think it's just a small, dirty pub. Yet, significantly, it's the first place Harry begins to realise that he's considered a celebrity among wizards and witches, and furthermore access to Diagon Alley is through the old courtyard at the back of the pub: all you have to do is find the brick that's three up and two across from the dustbin and tap it with your wand, and the archway will appear before you.

Diagon Alley is the high street for London's wizarding population with clothes shops (Madam Malkin's Robes for All Occasions), bookshops (Flourish and Blotts) and a sports shop (Quality Quidditch Supplies) as well as an apothecary's shop and an ice-cream parlour. There are also more unusual shops such as Ollivanders, where Harry buys his wand, an owl emporium and, on Knockturn Alley, Borgin and Burkes, a shop devoted to the Dark Arts.

Goblin-run Gringotts bank distributes and stores the wizarding currency – a gold Galleon is worth 17 silver Sickles, which are each worth 29 bronze Knuts.

Durham Cathedral is the location used for most of the shots of Hogwarts, Alnwick Castle is used during the flying lesson in *Harry Potter and the Philosopher's Stone* and Gloucester Cathedral is used for exterior shots. Number four Privet Drive is filmed at Martin's Heron in Bracknell, Berkshire and the Australian High Commission in London is the setting for Gringott's bank. Platform four at King's Cross station stands in for platform nine and three-quarters while the exterior of Harry Potter's King's Cross station is actually filmed at St Pancras.

How did Snape manage to fool Dumbledore?

After all the speculation over where Snape's loyalties really lie, it seems the latest bestseller has firmly placed him on the Dark side. Yet did Snape only kill Dumbledore because of the Unbreakable Vow spell that was cast over him? Was the look of disgust on his face actually an indication of the internal conflict within him? The brilliant and powerful wizard Dumbledore had taken the apparently reformed Snape on at Hogwarts in good faith and even finally granted him his wish to be the Defence Against the Dark Arts teacher, so why would Snape turn on him now? Professor McGonagall said that Dumbledore had reason to trust Snape, and there is a possibility that he allows his own murder as a sacrifice to save the lives of both Snape and Draco Malfoy. Did Dumbledore die so that one younger and stronger than himself could continue to help Harry?

Another school of thought proposes that Dumbledore did not in fact die: we did not see his body in the casket, and let's not forget the effect of the Polyjuice Potion, which enables someone to look like another person.

Harry Potter
and the Half-
Blood Prince

The Book

Harry finds an old textbook belonging to the Half-Blood Prince with scribbles that help him to excel in Potions. He's made Quidditch Captain and takes special lessons with Dumbledore during which they discover that Voldemort split his soul into seven pieces and placed six of the pieces into Horcruxes. Malfoy ambushes Harry and Dumbledore on the Astronomy Tower and Snape, the Half-Blood Prince, kills Dumbledore. Harry decides that he will not return to Hogwarts for his final year, but will search for the remaining four Horcruxes before finally confronting Voldemort.

The Latin phrase on the Hogwarts crest
means 'Never tickle a sleeping dragon'. It
is thought that J. K. Rowling may have
adapted this from the phrase 'Let sleeping
dogs lie'.

Horcruxes

A Horcrux is used to store part of a person's soul, keeping that part safe and thus affording a level of immunity to mortal death. The only way to detach part of your soul is to kill another human being; the ultimate act of evil. To create another Horcrux you must kill yet another person. Tom Riddle was so anxious to increase his power that he didn't hesitate in carrying out six murders in his quest to gain immortality.

While any object can be a Horcrux, Voldemort's vanity led him to choose objects with great significance - his mother's locket and his grandfather's ring both originally belonged to Salazar Slytherin and his diary contained proof that he was Slytherin's heir. He stole Helga Hufflepuff's cup from Hepzibah Smith, and it's possible that this, as well as objects from Godric Gryffindor and Rowena Ravenclaw, is also a Horcrux.

Although both the diary and the ring have been destroyed, Voldemort hasn't suffered the loss of those parts of his soul. He is still protected by the remaining Horcruxes, all of which are guarded by powerful enchantments, and he can only be defeated after all six have been eliminated.

Albus Percival Wulfric Brian Dumbledore

Professor Dumbledore has a very long silver beard, piercing, light blue eyes; and a scar in the shape of the London Underground on his left knee.

Sorted into Gryffindor, he was the Transfiguration teacher during Tom Riddle's school years and is now the Headmaster of Hogwarts. He lives at the top of one of the turrets at Hogwarts, through a door leading off from his circular office. Protected by a password that is always the name of a sweet, his office is accessed through the wall and up the moving staircase behind an ugly gargoyle.

A fan of tenpin bowling and chamber music, Dumbledore is also partial to sherbet lemons, a Muggle sweet not available in the wizarding world. 'Sherbet lemon' was one time, of course, a password for his office.

Hailed as one of the greatest wizards of the time for, among other things, his pioneering work with Nicolas Flamel, Dumbledore is the only wizard that Voldemort fears. Aware of Harry's destiny, he entrusted Harry to his aunt's care and has watched over him carefully since he heard Professor Trelawney's prophecy.

Magical Creatures

House-elves are servants in the wizarding community and carry out their duties without bringing attention to themselves. Bound to their masters, they cannot disobey them and cannot even speak ill of them. This extreme sense of loyalty leads to Winky's breakdown when she fails her master, Barty Crouch, and is banished from his employ. Dressed in tea towels, house-elves are freed when their masters give them clothes (even a smelly old sock will do).

The students are not allowed to enter the Forbidden Forest that surrounds Hogwarts because it's full of dangerous creatures such as centaurs and acromantulas. The small colony of centaurs is wary of

Muggles and wizards alike and prefers to live apart. They even attacked one member of their herd (Firenze) when he agreed to teach Divination after Professor Trelawney's dismissal. They are mysterious and intelligent half-human, half-equine beings with special interests in astronomy, divination, archery and healing.

Acromantulas are huge, spider-like creatures capable of human speech, bred by wizards to be guards. Hagrid befriended one, Aragog, during the year when the Chamber of Secrets was first opened. Aragog was blamed for Moaning Myrtle's death but survived because Hagrid released him into the Forest where he met his wife, Mosag, and they reproduced, creating spiders of all sizes.

Although Aragog considers Hagrid a friend and has never harmed him, he and his family would willingly (even eagerly) feast on human flesh and are a danger to anyone else who wanders into the Forest.

Another dangerous creature roaming around Hogwarts is the Basilisk, a gigantic green serpent with deadly venomous fangs and a stare which means instant death to anyone who looks into its eyes. A Basilisk is born when a chicken egg is hatched beneath a toad. Because of its snakelike characteristics, it communicates in Parseltongue, and obeys Tom Riddle's summons. It was the Basilisk that was responsible for Moaning Myrtle's death and for the petrification of several people during Harry's second year.

In the weeks leading up to the release of *Harry Potter and the Half-Blood Prince*, www.tesco.com reported that a copy of the book was ordered every 53 seconds – they sold 400,000 copies on the day the book was released. Bookscan announced that 2.01 million copies were sold in the UK during the first 24 hours while Scholastic sold 6.9 million copies in the US.

Rubeus Hagrid

Hagrid is a huge half-wizard, half-giant with long, wild hair and a great, shaggy beard. Despite his overbearing appearance, he is very gentle, and teaches the Care of Magical Creatures class with great enthusiasm. Even though he does have extensive knowledge of magical creatures, he is drawn to the dangerous ones, such as Hippogriffs and Blast-Ended Skrewts (his own experimental cross-breeding of manticores and fire-crabs). The most dangerous creature he has been involved with is his half-brother Grawp, a 'puny' sixteen-foot-tall giant. Most wizards consider giants to be barbaric and monstrous and would prefer if they remained in their mountain retreats. Hagrid is much loved among the Gryffindor students but he is a particular friend of Harry, Ron and Hermione. They have spent many a time in Hagrid's hut, drinking cups of tea and trying to get their teeth around his home-made rock cakes.

In his third year as a student at Hogwarts, Hagrid was expelled for a crime he did not commit. But Dumbledore never lost his faith in him and bestowed upon him the task of bringing Harry to the Dursleys' shortly after Voldemort's attack, as well as making him the Keeper of the Keys at Hogwarts.

Modes of Transport

Wizards have their own means of travel and rarely need to use Muggle transportation. Mr Weasley has a Ford Anglia but his additions (flying and invisibility enchantments, and an expanding boot to fit lots of luggage) set it apart from the average family car. The Knight Bus slides through traffic and jumps around the country to its passengers' desired destinations. The incantation *Portus* turns inanimate objects into Portkeys, which transport you to a different, specified location with just one touch; while travelling on the Floo Network is easy – one pinch of sparkling Floo powder thrown on the flames of a blazing fire enables wizards to travel from one fireplace to another.

Alternatively, after passing the required test (a necessary precaution because it's possible to get stuck between the places, leaving part of your body behind) a witch or wizard may transport him- or herself immediately from one place to another by Apparating.

Broomsticks are also popular, although they can be uncomfortable as the rider is more exposed to the elements and there is also the danger of being seen by a Muggle. Their most spectacular use is in the game of Quidditch, and Firebolts, Cleansweeps and Nimbus are just some of the brands available.

Charms

Wizards may have wands, but in order to make them work they need charms. As a witch's or wizard's skills develop, they can perform much more complicated charms but even the basic ones taught to first-year students at Hogwarts are helpful and used by the whole wizarding community.

The first charm Harry, Ron and Hermione learn in their Charms class is the Levitating Charm, when Professor Flitwick teaches the students to levitate a feather using their wands and the charm *Wingardium Leviosa*.

Other simple and very useful charms are *Lumos*, for creating light at the end of a caster's wand, and *Nox*, for turning it off, while the *Alohomora* charm opens locks and saves time hunting for keys. There are also charms for summoning objects (*Accio!*); for disarming opponents (*Expelliarmus*); and for Stunning people (*Stupefy*); as well as one (*Protego*) which creates a shield from the effects of other, not so friendly, charms.

Rupert Grint got the part of Ron Weasley in the films after performing a rap – unlike all the other hopefuls who read excerpts from the books.

Hy-Potter-sis

How will it all end?

With one book to go, we're left with more questions than ever before. Who is the mysterious R.A.B. and why didn't he, or indeed she, declare to the world how Voldemort could be defeated? Why didn't Dumbledore know about this person and enlist their help? It's possible that R.A.B. is Sirius's brother, so perhaps Harry will find something to help him destroy the Horcruxes in number twelve Grimmauld Place, which he recently inherited.

Why did Voldemort give Lily the chance to live? Could it be that Snape loved her and somehow convinced the Dark Lord to make an Unbreakable Vow to spare Lily's life? If so, then perhaps it was her murder and not his attack on Harry that caused his downfall. Will her sacrifice have any more repercussions for Harry?

Will we learn more about Harry's scar and the significance of him having his mother's eyes? When Lily died to save Harry's life, it could be that she poured part of her soul into the mark on his forehead, thereby protecting him forever.

How will the prophecy play out? Will Neville be involved? Is Harry capable of killing Voldemort? Harry is still a young wizard and although he will come of age very soon, he doesn't have the experience that Dumbledore had. It's possible that Harry won't be able to destroy the Horcruxes or will die in the attempt to kill Voldemort.

If Harry dies to save his friends and the rest of the magical world, could this be considered a happy ending? Though it would mean a short life for our hero, it could be considered that he had achieved his life's purpose in that time – perhaps a greater achievement than many could ever hope for. Will the boy who lived become the boy who died and saved them all?

Really Gross Facts

Everything you don't need to know but can't resist reading about

Ted Leech

£2.99 Pb

What grosses you out? How about this:

- Attila the Hun died from drowning in his own nosebleed.
- The best recorded distance for projectile vomiting is 27 feet.
- One pound of peanut butter can contain up to 150 bug fragments and five rodent hairs.

This crusty, thoroughly distasteful and utterly compelling book of facts will disgust your friends and give hours of revolting, sickening pleasure.

Bored Stupid!

Brainless things to do
when you're bored

A. Fidget

£2.99 Pb

Sand a mushroom... Ring McDonald's and complain about the food... Write a book about a previous life... Polish the ceiling... Plait your dog's hair... Wash a tree.

Bored to tears? On the bus, in a lecture, at home or at work, let's face it: life can be mindnumbingly boring sometimes.

Brighten up your drab and wholly pointless life with these brainless and completely daft things to do.

www.summersdale.com